The Complete

NOVICE

OBEDIENCE COURSE

by

BLANCHE SAUNDERS

Illustrated by Gloria Strang

Third Edition—Revised

1969

HOWELL BOOK HOUSE INC.

845 Third Avenue, New York, N. Y. 10022

THE NOVICE OBEDIENCE

TRAINING COURSE TEXTBOOK

TABLE OF CONTENTS

THE DOG FOR YOU

Owning the right dog is a pleasure. Owning the wrong one presents problems. If buying a dog is a new experience, before you buy, attend dog shows and talk with exhibitors. Ask about coat care and which breeds require professional clipping and trimming.

Talk with dog handlers and trainers. They work with all types of dogs and can tell you the breeds that are gentle and those that are more difficult to train. Discuss dogs with people who raise them, but don't expect an unbiased opinion. Kennel owners have their favorite breeds. Read books, magazines and dog publications. You will learn a lot through reading. Consult the "Selection Guide" in this book.

There are other ways you can learn about dogs. Inquire of your local Kennel Club about Puppy and Sanctioned Matches. Attend as a spectator. Talk with the neighborhood veterinarian. Most veterinarians are willing to answer "doggie" questions. Visit nearby kennels, but telephone first. Kennel owners have a busy schedule. Inquire at your local pet shops about free booklets that will tell you about dogs. Finally, ask those persons who already have a dog where they got theirs and what they like or dislike about their particular breed.

BUYING THE DOG

When it comes to buying the dog, The American Kennel Club, 51 Madison Ave., New York, N.Y., the national organization that specializes in purebred dogs, can advise you. Dogs are not kept on the premises, but the AKC, as it is called, will tell you about kennel owners and dog breeders.

Some dog clubs specialize in a single breed. If you are interested in one special kind of dog, write to the club secretary. You can find the name and address in dog magazines or dog show catalogs. The name and address will also be on record at The American Kennel Club.

A purebred dog may cost $100 or more, depending upon the popularity of the breed. Before buying a puppy, study the Standard for the breed so you will recognize good and bad features. For instance, two-colored Poodles are not accepted in the show ring. Neither are Boxers with too much white. Some breeds have to be a certain size. The Standard for **every** breed recognized in the United States is given in **The Complete Dog Book,** published by The American Kennel Club.

Before you decide on a puppy, visit different kennels. You may feel yourself drawn to one puppy more than another. While looking, don't expect to handle every puppy you see. Germs are easily carried from one kennel to another. Owners have to be cautious.

If you leave home with definite plans to get a dog, carry newspapers and towels for the return trip. Most puppies get carsick, although when you take a puppy riding every day, he should get used to the rock and roll of a motor car.

Take along a collar and leash. Nothing fancy. Just something that will get your puppy home safely if he is too big to hold in your arms.

Will it be a boy dog or a girl dog? The gentle, easy-to-handle female will cause inconvenience by coming in season but this can be overcome through spaying. Before you spay, let her develop, both mentally and physically. Spaying is usually done after six months of age and before the bitch comes in season the first time. (Remember that if you have the bitch spayed, she will be disqualified for competition in the breed ring.) If you want a dog with a more daring spirit, get a male, although males are apt to roam more and you have to watch their house manners. Where other dogs are concerned, males sometimes wear a chip on their shoulder, but either sex make good pets and good companions.

Think about age. The younger the puppy, the more quickly he will adjust to a new home. A six- or eight-weeks-old puppy requires extra care but when a puppy gets used to loud noises and unexpected situations early in life, he grows up a calmer adult dog.

Whether you buy from a kennel, from a pet shop, or from a private breeder (one who breeds his one or two pet dogs), ask questions:

Is the dog registered or eligible for registration with The American Kennel Club? You might want to breed, or to exhibit at dog shows.

What about inoculations? Write down the names of the shots that were given.

Ask when the puppy was last wormed and the kind of worms he had, if any.

Take note of health and general appearance. A healthy puppy will be active and full of play. His eyes will be bright and his coat shiny.

A puppy that cringes in the corner, is afraid of loud noises, and runs from people, is a shy puppy. Don't buy him. Shyness is hard to overcome.

All puppies are cute, but they don't stay puppies. Ask to see the parents so you will have some idea of what the puppy will look like when grown.

Ask what the puppy has been eating so you won't have to change his diet suddenly.

Request a copy of the puppy's pedigree through four generations, and, since some dogs change color when they mature, ask about a possible color change.

The final act will be the signing of the transfer slip or a paper for individual registration with The American Kennel Club.

BLANCHE SAUNDERS'
SELECTION GUIDE FOR DOG BREEDS

Successful training depends upon the breed, the age and the temperament of the dog, which is one way of saying that every dog can be trained, but certain factors, physical and otherwise, influence the ease of training and determine how pleasant a dog can be to live with.

Very small breeds, because of their size, seldom present a training problem. Even the most determined character is easily handled and can be made to obey. Small dogs can be yappier than large dogs; they can be quicker to nip and they do not hesitate to leave their calling card when they want to assert their authority. Small dogs appear to live longer.

Terrier breeds are characterized by their gameness and pep. Cocky and sure of themselves, with the instinct to unearth anything that moves, Terrier breeds make active, energetic companions. Eager and waiting, they are ready from the word "go."

When you see the word Spaniel, think of a sentimentalist. Gentle and easy-going, Spaniel breeds love everyone and they enjoy being fussed over. Spaniels and the other members of the Sporting Group—the Pointers, Setters and Retrievers—make wonderful hunting companions. Because of their instinct to point, flush or retrieve birds, Sporting breeds are apt to roam.

Hound breeds are of two kinds. Sight Hounds—such as the Greyhound, the Afghan Hound or the Saluki—track fur-bearing game by using their eyes. They are naturally quick-moving. Scent Hounds track man as well as other animals. They are slower moving and they instinctively have their nose to the ground. To train a Scent Hound

—such as the Bloodhound, the Bassett or the Beagle—to walk with his head in the air, can sometimes be a problem.

For guard work or herding, certain breeds perform better than others. Among the Working breeds, the German Shepherd Dog, the Doberman Pinscher, the Briard or the Giant Schnauzer are good examples of guard dogs. However, any large dog would be worth considering if you want a dog for protection. Size alone should frighten unwelcome intruders. So can the excessive barking of a small dog. For herding, the instinct is strong in Collies, Shetland Sheepdogs, Border Collies and Welsh Corgis.

Size is an important factor when buying a dog. Large dogs eat more than small dogs. There is the question of exercise and whether one has the ability to handle a dog of weight. But most large dogs are gentle and they make clean house pets.

Breeds with a short, flat, "pushed-in" nose will sniffle and snore more than breeds with a long head. Those with loose jowls will drool more than those with tight lips. Breeds with straight coats, whether long or short, unless the coat is of the wool variety, such as that of the Poodle or the Kerry Blue Terrier, will shed. Long hair requires grooming, and in the case of the Poodle and most Terrier breeds, unless you do the clipping or trimming yourself, there is the cost of professional coat care.

Will the dog live outdoors where he needs coat protection, or will he be a house-pet where coat is less important? Will he live in a hot climate where the Bulldog, for instance, might be uncomfortable? A Chihuahua, on the other hand, enjoys heat and sunshine.

The following guide will help you select your breed of dog. It rates each breed as a pet, with emphasis on size, care, temperament and training. Select your dog wisely.

VERY SMALL BREEDS	Weight: 4 to 12 pounds; height: 5 to 11 inches at top of shoulder back of neck. Recommended for apartment living, for people who travel and for those who want a lap dog. Exercise is no problem.
Affenpinscher	Bright, alert, friendly. Little grooming. Coat dense and wiry. Pert, Terrier spirit. Rare breed. Fearless toward aggressor.
Brussels Griffon	Easy to train. Little grooming. One coat variety smooth; one wiry. Reserved, sensitive nature. Hardy, spirited.
Chihuahua (Smooth)	Affectionate. Intelligent. Seldom roams. Short, glossy coat requires little grooming. Smallest of all dogs. Enjoys sunshine and heat. Slow to accept other breeds of dogs.
Chihuahua (Long-coated)	Affectionate. Not quarrelsome. Easy to train. Less clannish than the smooth variety. Coat long, silky, requires some grooming.
English Toy Spaniel	Extremely affectionate and good-tempered. Long, silky coat requires grooming.
Italian Greyhound	Gentle to care for. Calm, affectionate. Short, glossy coat requires little grooming. Seldom bathed. Not a yapper. One hardly knows there is a dog around unless his deep voice gives warning.
Japanese Spaniel	Well-mannered. Affectionate. Agile. Has definite likes and dislikes. Long, silky hair requires grooming.
Maltese	Lively, friendly, hardy. Adaptable to town or country. Long, silky hair requires extensive grooming.
Manchester Terrier (Toy)	Alert, clean house pet. Doesn't shed. Short, smooth coat.
Miniature Dachshund (Smooth) (Wirehaired) (Longhaired)	Responsive. Affectionate. Little grooming. Playful. Amusing. Longhaired variety requires some grooming.
Miniature Pinscher	Trains easily. Short, glossy coat requires little grooming. Good watch dog. Favors home and master.
Papillon	Anxious to please. Withstands both heat and cold. Excellent for country or city. Medium-short coat requires some grooming.
Pekingese	Bold, loyal, self-reliant. Faithful companion. Breed with definite likes and dislikes. Long, thick, silky coat requires extra grooming.

Pomeranian	A happy, alert, sturdy dog with stamina. Not quarrelsome. A guard dog that means business. Profuse, long, shiny coat requires extra grooming.
Toy Manchester Terrier	Alert. Clean house pet. Doesn't shed. Short, glossy coat requires little grooming.
Toy Poodle	Trains easily. Anxious to please. Companionable. No doggie odor. Doesn't shed. Upkeep expensive. Requires extensive grooming as well as professional clipping every 4 to 6 weeks.
Silky Terrier	Friendly. Spirited. Has sense of humor. Medium-long, silky hair requires grooming.
Yorkshire Terrier	Not a delicate lap dog. Highly intelligent. Possesses Terrier spirit and independence. Long, silky hair requires grooming.

SMALL BREEDS	Weight: 11 to 32 pounds; height: 9 to 20 inches. Suitable for small apartments. Exercise a minor factor.
Australian Terrier	Companionable. Easy to train. Harsh, wiry coat requires little grooming. Not a noisy dog.
Basenji	Clean house pet. While he doesn't bark, he does chortle. Short coat requires little grooming. Likes children. Playful, yet suspicious of the unusual.
Beagle	Good rabbit dog. Gentle, not quarrelsome. Short, flat coat requires little grooming. Sensitive nature. Like most Hound breeds, he always has his nose to the ground.
Bedlington Terrier	Quiet house pet. Doesn't shed. Affectionate. Fine, woolly coat requires special trimming.
Border Terrier	Friendly. Hardy, great courage and stamina. Harsh, dense, wiry coat requires little grooming. A fairly rare breed.
Boston Terrier	Sweet with people. Clean house pet. Short coat requires little grooming. Great home protector. Not yappy.
Cairn Terrier	Alert, adapts to town or country. Quieter than most Terriers. Profuse coat requires grooming but no professional trimming.
Cocker Spaniel	An alert family dog. As a rule, friendly toward both people and dogs. The silky, flat coat requires special trimming for show.
Dachshund **(Smooth)** **(Wirehaired)** **(Longhaired)**	Responsive. Lively. Playful. Amusing. Little grooming, except Longhaired variety, which requires some grooming. Somewhat a one-man dog.
Dandie Dinmont Terrier	Clean, obedient house pet. Intelligent. Patient with children. Medium-short coat requires some grooming but no professional trimming.
English Cocker Spaniel	A sensible fellow. Friendly. Affectionate. Flat, silky coat requires professional touch-up.
Fox Terrier **(Smooth)**	Friendly. Quick to learn. Smooth coat requires little grooming. A courageous, energetic sport. Good trick dog.
(Wire)	Good-natured toward people. Keen, sporty disposition. Requires professional trimming.
French Bulldog	Sweet-tempered, clean house pet. Short, smooth coat requires little grooming.
Irish Terrier	Country or city dog. Good with children. High spirited. Unflinching courage. Dense, wiry coat requires professional trimming.

Lakeland Terrier	Less excitable than most Terriers. Hard, dense, wiry coat requires professional trimming.
Lhasa Apso	Responsive. Trains easily. Good watch dog. Heavy, long coat requires extra grooming.
Manchester Terrier	Alert. Clean house pet. Doesn't shed. Short, smooth coat requires little grooming. One-man watch dog.
Miniature Poodle	Trains easily. Anxious to please. Companionable. No doggie odor. Doesn't shed. Upkeep expensive. Requires extensive grooming as well as professional clipping every 4 to 6 weeks.
Miniature Schnauzer	Companionable. Alert. Playful. Harsh, wiry coat requires professional trimming.
Norwich Terrier	Lovable. Not a quarrelsome breed. Dense, medium-short coat requires grooming but needs no trimming.
Pug	Friendly. Companionable. Clean house pet. Smooth, short coat needs little grooming.
Schipperke	Alert. Trains easily. Coat, while abundant, requires little grooming. Faithful watch dog.
Scottish Terrier	Devoted to master. Sturdy with independent disposition. Dense, wiry coat requires special trimming.
Sealyham Terrier	Friendly toward people and dogs. Intelligent. Has a sense of humor. Dense, harsh, wiry coat requires special trimming.
Shetland Sheepdog	Obedient and affectionate. Good with children. Loves family life. Delights in guarding property and giving warning. Medium-long, dense coat requires grooming.
Shih Tzu	Hardy. Town or country. Affectionate. Loyal. Alert. Small breed. Playful. Long, woolly coat requires grooming.
Skye Terrier	Possesses acute vision and hearing. Game-to-the-death Terrier. Long coat (5 to 6 inches) requires extensive grooming.
Welsh Corgi (Cardigan)	Good with children. Adapts to town or country. Dense coat requires little grooming.
(Pembroke)	Pleasing temperament. Responsive. Herding instinct.
Welsh Terrier	Not a quarrelsome breed. Likes town or country. Reliable with children. Wiry, close-fitting coat requires special trimming.
West Highland White Terrier	Friendly toward people and dogs. Hardy. Self-assured. Independent. Hard, stiff coat requires grooming but no professional trimming.
Whippet	Obedient. Untroublesome. Smooth, short coat. Little grooming. Never snappy or barky. One hardly knows there is a dog around.

MEDIUM-SIZED BREEDS	Weight: 35 to 60 pounds; height: 12 to 23 inches. Recommended for both country and city. Exercise is a factor.
Airedale Terrier	Friendly. Amiable playmate for children. Good family dog. Short, harsh, dense coat requires professional trimming. Fine guard dog.
American Water Spaniel	Good hunting companion. Fine family dog. Affectionate. Tightly curled coat requires some grooming.
Basset Hound	Friendly. Gentle. Short, dense coat. Little grooming.
Brittany Spaniel	Even-tempered. Companionable. Dense, flat coat requires little grooming. A hunting dog that both points and retrieves birds. Sensitive nature.
Bulldog	Reliable with children. Sweet with people. Patient. Flat, smooth coat.
Bull Terrier (White) (Colored)	Friendly toward people. Patient. Short, flat coat. Little grooming. Sensitive spirit. Powerful but amenable.
Chow Chow	Devoted to master. A one-man dog. Dense, woolly coat requires extra grooming.
Clumber Spaniel	Sedate. Lovable. Silky, dense coat, even with fringes, requires little grooming. Good hunting companion when speed is not essential. Rare breed.
Dalmatian	A versatile breed. Used for many purposes. Short, sleek coat. Little grooming. Not noisy. Carefree. Happy-go-lucky, yet capable of guard work.
English Springer Spaniel	A cheerful fellow. Friendly. Loving. Flat, medium-length coat requires little grooming. Professional trimming for show.
Field Spaniel	Friendly. Loving. Flat, silky hair requires little grooming. A hunting dog of moderate speed but great perseverance. Rare breed.
Harrier	Short, dense coat requires little grooming. A reliable hunting dog. Not a numerous breed.
Keeshond	Responsive. Anxious to please. Friendly. Likes children. Withstands cold. Sheds. Dense, thick coat requires grooming. Sensitive spirit.
Kerry Blue Terrier	Trustworthy with children. Doesn't shed. Soft, dense coat requires professional trimming.

Norwegian Elkhound	Sweet-tempered without nerves. Hardy. Courageous. Energetic. Thick, woolly coat requires grooming.
Puli	Gentle with children. Devoted, home-loving companion. A good watch dog. Long, fine hair requires extensive grooming.
Samoyed	Polite. Well-behaved. As in the case of all arctic breeds, no doggie odor. Good with children. Strong, alert, graceful. Thick, profuse coat requires grooming.
Siberian Husky	Friendly. Good for city or country. Free of doggie odor. Alert, graceful. Sled dog.
Standard Schnauzer	Sensible. Even-tempered. Good with children. Guard dog. Hard, wiry coat requires professional trimming for show.
Staffordshire Terrier	Reliable with children. Short coat. Little grooming. Powerful. Requires firm handling. Originally bred for fighting, now docile.
Sussex Spaniel	Pleasant. Companionable. Cheerful and tractable. A hunting dog. Flat coat with fringes requires some grooming.
Welsh Springer Spaniel	Amiable. Flat, silky coat. Little grooming. Retrieves both on land and water. Rare breed.
Wirehaired Pointing Griffon	Versatile. Easy-going. Hard, stiff coat. Little grooming. Not a numerous breed.
LARGE BREEDS	Weight: 55 to 75 pounds; height: 23 to 27 inches. Recommended for country living. For city living under certain conditions. Exercise a factor.
Afghan Hound	Withstands both heat and cold. Gentle by nature. Not snappish. Reserved. Prefers his own family. Not a noisy breed. Long, fine, silky hair requires extra grooming.
Alaskan Malamute	Gentle. Friendly. Woolly, thick, coarse coat requires little grooming. A sled dog, noted for pulling power and endurance.
American Foxhound	Friendly toward people. Short coat. Little grooming. A sporting dog with stamina.

Belgian Malinois	A large dog. Alert. Trainable for guard work. Devoted to master.
Belgian Sheepdog **Belgian Tervuren**	Alert. Devoted to master. Trainable for police work. Distrustful of strangers. Short to long, straight coat requires some grooming.
Bernese Mountain **Dog**	A good-natured "draft-horse." Withstands cold. Long, silky coat requires grooming. Little known breed.
Black and Tan **Coonhound**	Friendly. Gentle. Not quarrelsome. Short coat requires little grooming. A sporting dog that enjoys his work.
Boxer	Excellent with children. Clean house pet. Short coat. Little grooming. Playful. Suspicious of the unusual. Possesses rugged strength with ability to defend.
Briard	Has sharp sense of hearing and an unusually good memory. A family dog. Of a serious nature. Long coat requires grooming. Little bathing.
Chesapeake Bay **Retriever**	A retrieving dog that withstands rough, icy water. One of the best of all dogs with children. Powerfully built. Alert and willing to work.
Collie **(Rough)**	Friendly. Responsive. Trains easily. Not quarrelsome. Coat abundant. Requires care.
(Smooth)	Friendly. Responsive. Trains easily. Little coat care. Quite rare.
Curly-Coated **Retriever**	Willing. Trains easily. Sweet-tempered. Retrieves both from land and water. Dense mass of crisp, short curls requires grooming.
Doberman Pinscher	Trains easily. Smooth, short coat. Little grooming. Unafraid but mind their own business. Guard and police dog. Devoted to home and family.
English Foxhound	Affectionate. Responsive. Short, dense coat. Little grooming. Hunts as a part of a pack. As a pet, gentle.
English Setter	Gentle. Patient with children. Sensitive. Flat, silky coat requires professional "touch-up" for show.
Flat-Coated **Retriever**	Sensible. Obedient. Dense, flat coat. Little grooming. Retrieves both on land and water. Rare breed.
German Shepherd **Dog**	Intelligent. Devoted to family. Generally thought of as a "one-man" or "one-family" dog. Dense, close-lying coat requires some grooming.
German Shorthaired **Pointer**	Versatile sporting dog. Short coat. Little grooming. Mild manner. Not quarrelsome.

German Wirehaired Pointer	Companionable family dog. Harsh, wiry coat. Little grooming.
Giant Schnauzer	Intelligent. Willing. Close, strong, wiry coat. Little grooming. Used for guard and police work. Very reliable.
Golden Retriever	Gentle. Affectionate. Even-tempered. Trains easily. Good with children. Sheds a fair amount. Dense, water-resisting coat requires some grooming.
Gordon Setter	Gentle. Affectionate. Trains easily. One-man dog. Versatile as a sporting dog. Soft, silky coat with fringes, requires some grooming.
Greyhound	Gentle. Devoted. Short, smooth coat. Little grooming. Quiet in the home. One hardly knows there is a dog around.
Irish Setter	Gentle. Affectionate. Seldom resentful or aggressive. Happy-go-lucky. Carefree. Medium-short, flat, silky coat with fringes. Some grooming. Touch-up for show.
Irish Water Spaniel	Likable, all-round dog. Mass of tight, crisp, ringlets, requires grooming.
Kuvasz	Strongly home-loving. Seldom strays. Watch dog. Herd dog. Dense coat of medium length requires some grooming.
Labrador Retriever	Hardy. Devoted to people. Anxious to please. Short, dense coat. Little grooming. Powerfully built.
Old English Sheepdog	Excellent with children. Seldom fights. Seldom roams. Good for town or country. Has a sense of humor. Long, heavy coat requires extensive grooming.
Otter Hound	Sweet-natured. Wise. Hard, crisp, oily coat. Little grooming. Not a numerous breed.
Pointer	Works well for more than one master. Short, flat coat. Little grooming. Independent, alert. Has great stamina in the field.
Saluki	Affectionate. Withstands any climate. Little grooming. A quiet, lovable pet.
Standard Poodle	Trains easily. Anxious to please. Companionable. No doggie odor. Doesn't shed. Upkeep expensive. Requires extensive grooming as well as professional clipping every 4 to 6 weeks. Excellent with children.
Vizsla	A large dog with an excellent nose. Coat short, smooth. Bird dog of moderate speed.
Weimaraner	Intelligent. Energetic. Short, smooth coat. Little grooming. A hunting dog with great power and stamina.

VERY LARGE BREEDS	Weight: 90 to 185 pounds; height: 25 to 33 inches. Recommended for country living. Exercise a major factor.
Bloodhound	Gentle. Affectionate. Short, smooth coat. Little grooming. "Sniffy"—that's his job!
Borzoi	Gentle. Graceful. Quiet. Light on leash. Long, silky coat requires grooming.
Bouvier des Flandres	Level-headed. Capable. Tousled short coat requires little grooming. Rare breed in United States.
Bullmastiff	Sensible. Short, dense coat. Little grooming. Guard dog. Gives protection without savagery.
Great Dane	Friendly toward people. Short, smooth coat. Little grooming. Spirited, courageous, dependable.
Great Pyrenees	A home-loving dog. Sweet with people. Especially children. Intelligent. Guard dog. Thick, heavy coat requires grooming.
Irish Wolfhound	A peaceful house pet. Courteous and gentle. Even-tempered. Devoted. Tallest of all breeds. A quiet dog. Wiry, harsh coat. Some grooming.
Komondor	Self-reliant. Guard dog. Distrustful of strangers. Woolly coat requires extra grooming. Not a numerous breed.
Mastiff	Devoted family dog. Good-natured, courageous, docile. Short coat. Little grooming. Heaviest of all breeds.
Newfoundland	Lovable, gentle. Responsive. Intelligent. The canine "lifeguard." Heavy, dense, oily, water-proof coat requires grooming.
Rhodesian Ridgeback	Devoted family dog. Never noisy or quarrelsome. Short, flat coat. Little grooming. The hair grows the wrong way in a ridge down the back. Not so well-known as some other breeds.
Rottweiler	Affectionate. Obedient. Steady disposition. Short coat. Little grooming. Guard dog. Herder.
St. Bernard	Gentle with people. Has an uncanny sense of smell and of approaching danger. Dense, moderately long, flat coat requires grooming.
Scottish Deerhound	Devoted, polite, pleasant house pet. Desires human companionship. Harsh, wiry coat (3 to 4 inches) requires grooming.

SOME OF THE LESSER KNOWN BREEDS MORE RECENTLY APPROVED BY THE AMERICAN KENNEL CLUB

Akita	Short, dense coat. Little grooming. A large dog used for herding.
Australian Heeler	Herding dog of medium size.
Australian Kelpie	Abundant, long, hard coat. Some grooming. Small herding dog.
Border Collie	Obedient. Alert. Agile. Herding dog of medium size, with stamina.
Cavalier King Charles Spaniel	Extremely affectionate. Good tempered. Long, silky coat requires grooming.
Chinese Crested Dog	Bright. Affectionate. Agile. No coat care. Similar to Hairless Mexican. Very small. Lack of hair on the body, not always appealing.
Russian Owtchar	Hair, short to long and straight. A very large, courageous dog.
Soft-Coated Wheaten Terrier	Small breed. Coat soft and wavy. Farm and sporting dog.
Spinoni Italiana	Withstands all weather. Coat rough. Short. Little grooming. Dog of medium size.

THE PUPPY'S EARLY TRAINING

A well brought up dog is obviously more pleasant to have around than one that can only be termed a general nuisance. Yet, the majority of dog owners neglect their dog's **early** education, so vital to good upbringing. Dogs by the hundreds of thousands chase automobiles, keep neighborhoods awake with senseless barking, leap with dirty paws on immaculate guests, bite delivery boys and postmen, ruin furniture, and make walking them on a leash a tense, tangled, arm-straining ordeal.

Teaching a dog to behave is really not hard or complicated. All it normally requires is patience, an understanding of the dog, and simple training techniques that follow a basic pattern.

HOW DOES A DOG LEARN?

A dog learns, not through her * rudimentary reasoning power, but by associating pleasant or unpleasant consequences with her behavior. She obeys commands or signals when they are connected with such associations in her mind. And after the trainer repeats the commands or signals often enough for the dog's reactions to become habitual, the dog may properly be termed obedient.

A dog is best educated through praise and gentle scolding, and through the proper use of the collar and leash for routine obedience training. Tell the average dog what you want, and when you help her to obey, she will cooperate willingly. It is only the problem dogs that require special handling. But in any case, correcting or disciplining must be done at the time or immediately after the dog errs so she will understand the reason for the punishment. She must be corrected every time the mistake is made so she will associate the punishment with her act.

* Note: Throughout this book the dog is referred to as **her,** in the interest of simplicity. This does not mean that male dogs are poor performers or any more difficult to train than females.

WHEN SHOULD TRAINING BE STARTED?

The dog training may be started as early as four or five months of age, but before we get into formal education, here are some things every puppy should learn:

To Stay Alone Quietly

Whether you acquired your puppy at six weeks or at four months of age, teach her to stay by herself. Shut her in a room, then close the door. If she barks or scratches to get out, toss something at the door that will make a loud noise. If the barking or scratching continues, toss it again. Do this at intervals until the puppy will learn to stay by herself without making a fuss. After the puppy gets used to daytime solitude, she will adjust more quickly to staying alone at night. A dog that hasn't been trained to stay alone will usually bark, chew, or deliberately wet when you leave her.

Not To Jump On People

While committed in the friendliest of spirits, one of dogs' most irritating social errors is jumping on people. Every time your puppy comes running, spread your fingers fan-like and say "NO

JUMPING!" If she jumps up in spite of the warning, bump her nose once to make her get down. Then pat her. You can also lift your knee when your dog jumps up, but the spread fingers with the warning "No jumping!" is more effective.

To Keep Off Furniture

Start by pushing the puppy down every time she tries to get on the furniture. Use a stern "NO!" If she sneaks up when you are out of the room, place something in her favorite chair that will squawk or make some other loud noise. A wound-up toy or a crackly paper should do the trick.

Not To Steal Food

Leave food where the puppy can reach it. When she tries to sniff it, call out sharply "NO!" If necessary, tap her gently on the nose to remind her. If the habit still persists, toss something so it lands close to the food she is reaching for. One or two experiences should cure the habit of stealing.

Not To Chase Cars

If you are driving the car, stop and chase the puppy home. If this is ineffective, carry two or three small empty cartons in the car and while chasing her, toss the cartons in back of her. If the puppy is broken to collar and leash, work with a friend. Ask the friend to blast the car horn when he approaches, then forcefully jerk the puppy away from in front of the car so she will learn to respect moving vehicles.

Not To Chew, Bark, Or Wet

Chewing, barking, and wetting in the house are cured more quickly when you catch the puppy doing wrong. The first few times, call out sharply "NO!" and stop her from doing mischief. If she persists in spite of the warning, drop some small object close by and surprise her in the act. A wire cage, available at most kennel supply shops, where you can keep the puppy when you can't watch her, will simplify raising a young puppy. Learning to stay quietly alone in her own little house is an important part of a puppy's training. She will also be where she can't do damage.

SIMPLE OBEDIENCE TRAINING (FOUR TO FIVE MONTHS)

Begin simple training by introducing the puppy to her collar—a leather one—and her leash. Play with her. Let her drag the leash on the ground. Avoid the unpleasantness resulting from jerking the leash too hard or forcefully dragging the puppy around.

Lesson 1. Walking Without Pulling On The Leash

Don't expect your young puppy to ALWAYS walk at heel position as required in Obedience Trials, but teach her to walk **without pulling.** Every time she darts ahead, say "Heel!" (she might as well learn this word from the beginning), tug backward on the leash, then pat your side to encourage her to walk there. If she darts ahead a second time, stand still and repeat the action. When she walks with leash slack, praise her, and tell her, "Good girl!"

If the puppy won't walk at all, kneel and tap your fingers on the ground. Coax her with praise. If she still refuses to walk, **slowly** and **gently** drag her while you give continuous praise. When the puppy no longer grovels but gets to her feet, slacken the leash and clap your hands for encouragement.

Lesson 2. The Sit

When you want your puppy to sit, hold her head up with the leash in one hand, say "Sit!" and while you push on her hindquarters with the other hand to make her sit, tell her "Good Girl!" After she is sitting, pat her.

Later, instead of pushing on the hindquarters, tap them lightly to make her sit more quickly. Remember to say "Sit!" before you spank her to a sitting position, so she will learn the meaning of the word.

Lesson 3. Staying When Told

A young puppy won't stay for long when the owner is some distance away. She can, however, be taught to stay on the grooming table or to stay on command the length of the leash. Put the puppy on a low bench or table and tell her "Stay!" If she tries to jump off, put her back and tell her "Stay!" again. When she gets off the table, it should be with your permission.

For leash training, with the puppy sitting at your left side, place your left hand in front of her muzzle and tell her "Stay!" After you say it, step forward on your right foot. If she follows, grab the leash and quickly put her back where she was. If she stays when you tell her, turn and face her, then slowly circle to your right, around and in back of her. At first you may have to use both hands to keep her sitting.

Lesson 4. Coming When Called

The object here is to teach the puppy the meaning of the word "Come!" This is accomplished through timing the command with the use of the leash, then giving a generous reward for coming. With the puppy on leash, call her name and tell her "Come!" whether she is looking at you or not. After you call, tug once on the leash, then clap your hands to encourage her to come quickly. If you are working with a small dog, kneel when you call her. Do this until your puppy will turn and run toward you when she hears you call.

Lesson 5. To Lie Down

Avoid roughness when you make your puppy lie down. Move slowly and handle gently. There are different ways you can make a puppy lie down. You can pull down on the collar and press lightly on her shoulders or hindquarters. You can trip the puppy by turning both her back legs to one side to make her lie on one hip. You can reach over the puppy's back and slide the front legs forward. The important things to remember: give the command first, and while you are putting the puppy down slowly, praise her or scratch her gently with your fingers.

Lesson 6. To Stand

With the puppy on leash, pull the leash **forward** with one hand while you tickle her under the stomach with the other. At the same time, say "Stand!" After she is standing, scratch her back and if she tries to sit down, reach under her stomach and lift her gently. A dog that learns to stand on command is easier to groom.

THE NOVICE OBEDIENCE COURSE

Four Important Reasons Why Your Dog Should Be Trained:

1. For your own pleasure, comfort, and satisfaction
2. For your dog's happiness, well-being, and safety
3. To avoid annoyance to your friends and neighbors
4. For the good of your community

A trained dog may be qualified to enter Obedience Trials at dog shows and win Obedience Degrees.

A TRAINED DOG IS A HAPPY DOG!

THE DOG IN TRAINING

The dog in training should be in good physical condition and given the necessary inoculations to safeguard health.

Before each training session:

Feed lightly

Exercise

Give a small amount of water

Groom, for both comfort and appearances' sake

Having attended to your dog's needs, be serious, but not domineering, about the training.

Dog training is divided into two phases: (1) teaching, and (2) employing corrective techniques to overcome problems. There is no **one** way to train a dog, nor do two dogs react to training in exactly the same way, but owners who are interested in training their dogs for Obedience competition should keep the following in mind : during basic training, first consideration should be for the dog and not the rule book. After the dog has learned to work happily and with spirit, the handler should condition himself for the Obedience ring by eliminating double commands, body motions and extra praise used while teaching. When making corrections, he should also keep in mind that the manner in which corrections are made is what counts.

TRAINING SUGGESTIONS

When you teach voice commands, give the command then follow with the **signal,** and the **correction** and the **praise** simultaneously.

When you teach hand signals, give the signal then follow with the **voice,** and the **correction** and the **praise** together.

When you want your dog to come, call her name, give the command and follow the command with **praise.** While she is coming, clap your hands to cheer her on.

When your dog is some distance away and you want her to obey a command (for instance, to stay), stress the command without using her name. The name may bring her to you.

Give a command ONCE! If you repeat the command, put a correction with it.

Praise must be discontinued when exhibiting in Obedience Trials but if used AFTER every command and WITH every correction during the training period, your dog will be more responsive.

When you praise, BE SINCERE! Dogs respond to a cajoling tone of voice.

Modify your method of training to the SIZE AND TEMPERAMENT of the dog. All dogs do not train alike!

When you correct for a problem, disguise corrections so you, the trainer, will not appear responsible.

Don't overdo corrections. Start gently until you see how YOUR dog reacts.

If your training efforts are NOT successful, be more demanding. When you correct for a REPEATED mistake, use a firmer tone of voice and jerk the leash harder.

Strive for perfection from the beginning. When you are careless about little things, they become problems later on.

If you are a woman and prefer to train in a dress, select one without too much flare. Training a small dog necessitates stooping or bending. A full skirt will get in the dog's way.

In Obedience Trials, you cannot use your dog's name when you give a hand signal. In other words, you cannot say "Robin!" and motion your dog to come or to go-to-heel. In your early training, avoid using your dog's name when you give a signal.

You cannot give a hand signal with a voice command EXCEPT when you leave your dog alone. In this case, you can say "Stay!" and make a motion with your hand, but you CANNOT say "Robin, stay!" and give the signal.

At the start of heeling and after every halt, use your dog's name with the heeling command to get her attention.

Condition your dog for the Open Course by encouraging her, during basic training, to carry assorted articles, to retrieve thrown objects, and to leap small hurdles. This early training paves the way for the advanced work, without affecting the dog's skill while competing in the Novice Classes.

The instructions given in the succeeding sections of this book are for people who are right-handed. Those who are left-handed may follow the same instructions, simply substituting the left hand for the right and the right hand for the left.

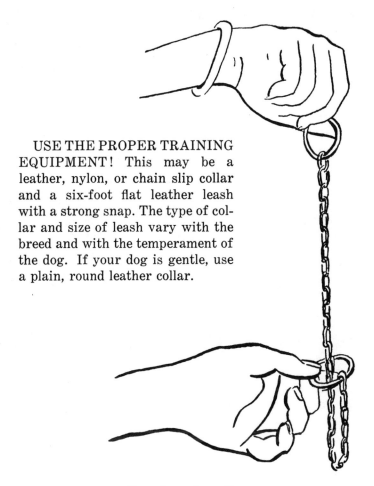

USE THE PROPER TRAINING EQUIPMENT! This may be a leather, nylon, or chain slip collar and a six-foot flat leather leash with a strong snap. The type of collar and size of leash vary with the breed and with the temperament of the dog. If your dog is gentle, use a plain, round leather collar.

How to make collar

PRACTICE HOW TO HOLD THE LEASH! Loop the handle around the palm of your right hand and take hold of the leash with the left hand, above the dog's head. Bring your right hand to your waist and grasp the leash in the center. Hold both arms close to the body and keep the left elbow straight. (See illustration.)

When you hold the leash this way, you can make heeling corrections with a minimum of hand motion.

LEARN HOW TO PUT ON THE SLIP COLLAR! With the dog on your left side, the leash fastens to the ring of the chain that passes OVER the dog's neck. If on correctly, the collar will click when you snap the leash and will loosen when you slacken it. (See illustrations.)

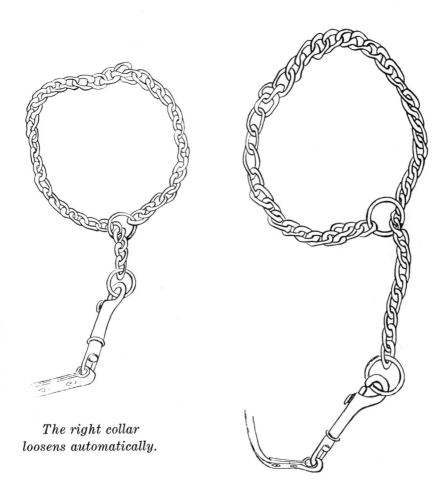

The right collar loosens automatically.

The wrong collar stays tight all the time.

Note: in Obedience Trials a dog is required to walk at the handler's left.

THE TRAINER

KEEP YOUR DOG'S ATTENTION. Play with her! Nudge her when she looks away. Make unexpected turns while heeling.

DON'T LET YOUR DOG BE "SNIFFY." Tug on the leash every time she lowers her head or tries to sniff other dogs.

DON'T LET YOUR DOG LUNGE AT ANOTHER DOG. Threaten her with a small, rolled magazine. If it is a small dog you are training, drop the magazine at her feet.

DON'T LET YOUR DOG BARK UNCONTROLLED. Pull the collar tight and cuff her nose. In persistent cases, muzzle with a piece of 2-inch gauze bandage.

TIME YOUR CORRECTIONS. Tell your dog what you want, then use the leash to help her do it.

CORRECT WITH A MINIMUM OF HAND MOTION. Don't **drag** on the leash. Snap it!

USE THE PROPER TONE OF VOICE—a normal tone for first commands, a demanding tone (without yelling) when the dog disobeys.

KEEP YOUR DOG HAPPY. Give praise after every command and every time you use the leash. If you train in a rough manner, it will show in your dog's attitude.

*A tap on the hindquarters with the right
foot will keep your dog attentive.*

HEELING

With the leash in both hands (with the left elbow straight and both arms close to your body), command "Robin, heel!" **After you give the command,** move forward on your left foot, snap the leash forward, pat your side and give praise. Timing and praise are important! If your dog darts ahead, STAND STILL. Snap the leash backward, again giving praise. Make left U-turns every few feet (both handler and dog turn to the left), and if your dog still forges, lift your knee and bump her chest. If it is a small dog you are training, use the inside of your right foot to push her around on the turns. Praise when you make these corrections.

Alternate the left U-turn with the right-about turn. Pivot sharply **without slackening speed and without dragging on the leash.** After you turn, snap the leash forward, then again pat your side.

Include a fast and a slow pace in the heeling exercise. When you run, jerk the leash forward **with praise.** When you slow to a walk, jerk the leash backward, giving praise. Use short, quick snaps.

Circle continuously to the right, then circle continuously to the left. Follow the circling with a zigzag pattern. A change of direction will keep your dog attentive.

By now the heeling routine should include right-angle and left-angle turns. Pivot sharply without slackening speed and tug on the leash **after** you turn. Practice the Figure 8. Circle two posts, two chairs, or two of anything, placed 6 to 8 feet apart. Teach your dog to change pace as you did in the heeling exercise (see above). Do this by speeding up when the dog is on the outside of the circle, and jerking the leash forward in a series of snaps while giving praise. Slow to a walk when the dog is on the inside of the circle, then speed up again when she is on the outside, this time without jerking the leash. Give praise as before.

Continue the heeling routine with the handle of the leash over your shoulder and with your arms at your side. WALK BRISKLY! Never adapt your pace to that of the dog. At the first sign of carelessness, use a demanding "HEEL!" and jerk the leash harder. Follow corrections with a few words of praise.

When heeling with the leash over the shoulder is nearly perfect, permit your dog to heel free. Carry the leash, wadded up, in your right hand. Hold your left hand close to your side and encourage the dog by gently patting your thigh. If your dog stays close and heels nicely, let her know you are pleased by praising her while she is working. If she breaks away, STAND STILL. Use a demanding tone when you repeat the heeling command and if she still ignores it and starts running around, throw the leash at her heels to make her listen. Kneel, and tell her "COME!" After she comes, snap the leash on her collar, and make sharper corrections.

If you are working with a large dog that is slow to come around on the about-turn, put the dog on leash. Wad the handle of the leash into a ball and carry it in your left hand. When you make the about-turn, reach back with your right hand and spank the dog playfully on the rump. After you spank her, clap your hands so the dog will think the correction was in fun. If you do it carefully, you can use your right foot instead of your hand, but don't make the correction too often.

When teaching your dog to heel, make the training a game. Use playful corrections when possible and give adequate praise so your dog will enjoy the heeling exercise.

Lags While Heeling

Put the dog on leash and make corrections whether you think the dog needs them or not. In other words, don't go through the heeling routine just holding the leash. After every change of direction and change of pace, snap the leash forward, giving praise. Do this two or three times, then give praise when you turn, without jerking the leash.

If temperament permits, an assistant can sometimes walk behind the dog and gently tap her with a light rod every time she drops back. Tapping the floor with the rod will sometimes speed up a lagging dog. After these corrections, the owner must encourage the dog to stay close through praise and patting.

Wide On The Right-About Turn

With your dog on leash and sitting at heel position, do a series of about-turns from a standstill. When you turn, reach back with your **right** foot and tap the dog gently on her right flank. Halt, and immediately pat her. If you are working with a small dog, assume a crouched position in order to have the hands on level with the dog. During the heeling routine, pivot sharply and do a complete circle to the right. When the leash is off, make playful corrections by spanking the large dog on the rear.

Dog Heels On Wrong Side

When the dog comes in on the wrong side, reach back with your **right** hand and cuff her once on the nose. Pat your left leg with your left hand to encourage her to come there. If you are working with a small dog, carry something firm but soft, that will just clear the floor. Instead of using your hand, use the object to bump her nose.

Fails To Change Pace

Put the dog on leash. When you run, jerk the leash forward, giving praise. Slow down to a walk, then dash forward again.

HEELING Problems—How To Overcome Them

After two or three corrections, go into the running pace without jerking the leash, but give praise just as before. Hold your hands close to your body to avoid excessive arm motion.

Barks While Heeling

If the dog barks while on leash, tug on the leash forcefully and tell her "STOP!" If she barks off leash, carry something that you can throw at her feet, or have an assistant throw it. Most dogs bark when they do an exercise fast. Repeat the correction until your dog will go into a running pace without yapping.

Lags On The Figure 8

Repeat the exercise suggested in the training instructions. Hold the leash in **both** hands if it is a large dog, and in the left hand if it is a small dog. When the dog is on the inside of the circle, walk naturally. When she is on the outside, speed up and jerk the leash forward in a series of snaps, giving praise. The third or fourth time around, speed up without jerking the leash but give praise just the same. This will teach your dog to change pace, an important feature of the Figure 8.

Forges While Heeling

An assistant walks at the dog's left and holds the leash in BOTH hands if it is a large dog, or in the right hand if it is a small dog. The owner gives the heeling command and follows the command with praise. Each time the dog forges, the owner repeats the word "heel." The assistant then jerks the leash backward with force.

An assistant can walk backward in front of the owner who is heeling his dog. When the dog forges, the assistant can bang on the floor (if it is a wooden floor) with some object held in his hand, or drop something, such as a small empty carton, in front to block the dog.

HEELING Problems—How To Overcome Them

Dog Bites Hand Or Leash While Heeling

If it is a large dog, hold your left hand still. When the dog misbehaves, cuff her nose with the right hand. Tell her "Stop it!" If it is a small dog and she bites at the leash, shake the leash hard or tap her on the nose and tell her "Stop!"

Dog Jumps Up And Down While Heeling

Every time the dog jumps up, use the leash to throw her off balance. When all four feet are on the ground, praise and pat her.

Dog Springs At Handler, Growling And Biting

Handle calmly. Take the leash in BOTH hands. Hold the dog away from your body and lift the front feet off the ground. After she quiets down, command "Sit," then quietly pat her.

Avoid jerking the leash. Drag the dog *slowly*, giving continuous praise. While she takes a few steps, slacken the leash but continue with the praise. In stubborn cases, lean over and tap the ground or the floor as you pull the dog toward you.

Patting the hip encourages the dog after leash corrections.

An assistant helps train a dog to stay at heel

THE SIT

When you come to a halt, shorten the leash in your **right** hand. Pull the leash **up** and **backward.** Push down on the dog's hindquarters with the left hand. Say "Sit, good girl (or boy) !" Pat her with the same hand you used to push her to the sitting position.

If your dog braces herself and you haven't the strength to force her to sit, flip the handle of the leash across her rump, and after she is sitting, pat her.

After she knows the meaning of "Sit," make her sit quickly. "Spank" her to a sitting position, then pat her with the same hand you used to spank her. The dog may think you are generous with your praise, but you will get excellent results.

During the heeling routine, wad the handle of the leash into a ball and hold it in your left hand, with the left elbow straight. When you halt, bring your feet together but don't move your left arm. Wait and see what the dog does. If she passes your knee without sitting, snap the leash backward. If she continues to stand, spank her to a sit. If she sits without being corrected, praise her. Give her credit for doing a good job. In Obedience Trials, the dog must sit when you halt, without being told. Each time you correct for not sitting, make the correction harder.

Don't step into your dog when you halt. This will make her move away. If she sits wide, coax her to come close. If she sits at an angle, straighten her out! The sit should be square and facing straight ahead.

Teaching the SIT

THE SIT-STAY
(The Long Sit)

Now that your dog knows how to sit, practice the sit-stay. With your dog at heel position, hold your left hand in front of the dog's muzzle, say "Stay!" and step forward on your right foot. Don't use your dog's name. If she follows, cuff her once, gently, on the nose (if she is a large dog), or use the leash to jerk her back to a sitting position. Repeat the command in a more demanding tone of voice.

When you leave your dog, give the stay signal with the left hand. Hold the palm toward the dog's muzzle with fingers pointing to the floor. When you face your dog, turn your hands so the palms are again toward the dog's muzzle with fingers pointing down. With the hands in this position you can quickly correct any forward movement with a cuff under the chin or use the leash to jerk the dog backward to make her sit down.

Holding the leash, circle your dog several times while she is sitting. Return to heel position by going to your right and around in back of the dog. Hold the leash to your left so it doesn't wrap itself around the dog. If your dog moves before you give permission, repeat the command more demandingly, and when you correct, correct rather sharply. At first, you may have to use both hands to keep her sitting. Do not yell and do not become angry.

With your dog sitting, tell her "Stay!" Face her, and then try to pull her from the sitting position. Don't jerk the leash, just pull it taut. Your dog should settle back and refuse to move. If she does move, correct her with a gentle cuff under the chin and tell her again, "Stay!"

While practicing the sit-stay, stand behind your dog as well as in front of her. It is permissible for a dog to turn her head but not her body. Try putting the leash on the ground but keep it fastened to the dog's collar. If she moves without permission, step on the leash, grab it up quickly and put her back where she was. At the same time, change your tone of voice to a demanding "STAY!"

Take the leash off. Increase the distance and the length of time you leave the dog. Tempt her by running past her. Clap your hands or call to another dog. If she moves, correct her. Leave her in the sit-stay position while you prepare her dinner or load the car for an outing. Try going where she can't see you. All of these things will help make your dog reliable on the sit-stay.

Hand signal STAY from the side

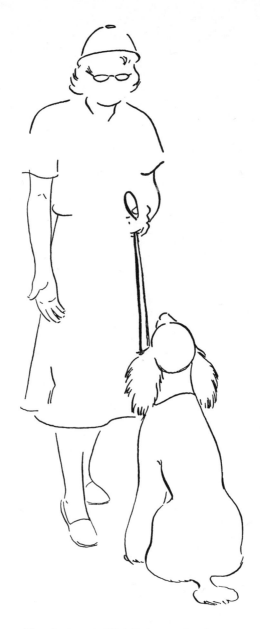

Hand signal STAY from the front

Feet should be together before you correct for slow sits or for sitting ahead.

SIT AND SIT-STAY Problems—How To Overcome Them

Slow To Sit On The Halt

While heeling, wad the handle of the leash into a ball and hold it in your left hand. Keep the elbow straight. Come to a halt and **after** your feet come together, jerk the leash backward with force, to make the dog sit quickly. Give praise at the same time. The important thing is to have no motion of the feet at the time you jerk the leash.

Alternate correction: an assistant walks at the dog's left. After the owner halts, the assistant spanks the large dog to a sitting position, to make her sit faster. He taps the small dog more gently. Both assistant and handler give praise.

Sits Ahead

Same as "Slow To Sit On The Halt."

Lies Down During The Sit-Stay

Fasten a long line to the dog's collar. Run the line through a ring placed four or five feet above the dog. Ask an assistant to stand off to one side and hold the end of the line. When the dog starts to lie down, a tug on the line will bring her to a sitting position.

To correct the dog that lies down when the leash is off, saunter back until you are directly in front of the dog, then quickly reach out with your foot and tap or scuff into the front paws. When the dog is sitting, praise and pat her.

If your dog lies down on a slippery floor, try sliding something along the floor underneath her to make her jump to a sitting position. Say "Sit!"

*A tap on the rear with a small, rolled magazine
will speed up a large dog that is slow to sit.*

SIT AND SIT-STAY Problems—How To Overcome Them

Sits At An Angle

An assistant walks at the dog's left. If the dog swings her hindquarters away from the handler, the assistant taps the dog gently on her left hip to make her sit straight. The hand or a light rod can be used to tap the dog, but praise must be given with the correction.

If the crooked sit is in the opposite direction, reach back with your right foot and gently tap the dog's right hip to make her straighten out.

Both Heels And Sits Wide

With the dog on leash, walk her close to a wall or a fence. If she heels wide and bumps into the barrier, she may correct herself of this habit, especially if you encourage her to come close by patting your leg. If she veers away and won't be coaxed to sit close, avoid jerking the leash. Hold it tight and pull her to you, then tell her "Sit!" Wide heeling and sitting are usually the result of jerking the leash without adequate praise. They also result from grabbing at the dog while heeling, or from stepping into the dog when you halt.

Refuses To Sit And Stay

Put your dog on a long line and ask an assistant to hold the end of the line, some distance in back of the dog, or tie it to a stationary object. After you tell your dog "Stay," face her. Watch her carefully. Then kneel down, which may tempt her to break. If she does, call out from the distance, "STAY!" after which the assistant gives one jerk on the leash. Take the dog back and try again. This time you may have to clap your hands to get her to move. Try playing with another dog. The important thing is to tempt your dog to move so you can call out "STAY," from the distance, before the line checks her.

THE COME FORE AND THE GO-TO-HEEL POSITION
(The Finish)

While heeling your dog, walk backward and say, "Robin, come fore," "Come front," or just plain "Come!" When she turns to face you, bring her close by holding both hands under her chin and pulling the leash toward you. Give praise at the same time. After she comes close, command "Sit!" Then pat her. If she isn't sitting straight, square her up before you pat her.

With the dog now sitting facing you, say "Robin, heel," and walk past her to your right. Give the leash a tug as you go by, pat your side, and after the dog turns around, halt. Then pat her.

Next, to make the go-to-heel position easier, get the dog on her feet after you give the command. Bring her in front in the usual way by walking backward and telling her "Come!" After she is sitting in front, tell her "Robin, heel!" Then pull her to a standing position by taking two steps backward. After she is on her feet, take two steps forward to make her turn around. When you step back, pull on the leash and give praise. When you step forward, pat your knee to encourage her to turn around.

Next, pretend the right foot is glued to the floor or fastened to the ground. Only the left foot moves. After you say "Robin, heel!" take a big step backward with your left foot and guide the dog around to your left side with your left hand. Hold your hand under her chin. Take a big step forward with the same foot, as you pat your left leg to coax the dog to face front. Move the right foot only when necessary.

Try for a quick response to your command. After you give the command, snap the leash hard, give praise, then pat your side for encouragement. If your dog moves around to your side when she hears the command "Heel" or sees the hand move, don't jerk the leash but give praise as usual. The praise will help bring her around.

If you prefer to train your dog to go to the right and around in back, follow the same procedure in reverse. Give the command first. Follow by using the leash and giving praise for encouragement.

Teach your dog to go to heel position on signal. With the dog on leash, sitting facing you, hold the leash in your right hand. Drop your left hand as a signal to go to the left side. After you drop your hand, reach for the leash with the same hand and bring the dog around. Do this often enough and your dog will start for your left side when your hand starts to move.

Note: in Obedience Trials a dog is permitted to go to heel position by going to the right and in back of the handler. For the purpose of teaching, the left-side method of going to heel position will be used.

FINISH Problems—How To Overcome Them

Sloppy Finishes

In practice, hold the handle of the leash wadded into a ball, in your left hand. Do a series of:

1) Steps to the right
2) Quarter-turn pivots to the left
3) About-turns from a standstill
4) A step to the rear

With each change of direction, command "Heel!" Then snap the leash to make the dog assume the correct heel position. Give praise when you jerk the leash.

Ignores Command To Go To Heel

Put the dog on leash. Without moving your hands or your feet, command "Heel!" Then, if you are training a large dog, with BOTH hands jerk the leash to your left side and as far back as you can reach. Give praise and pat your knee to turn the dog and make her face front. When training a small dog, lean over so your hands are level with the dog. Use only the left hand to jerk the leash, and do it more gently.

In stubborn cases, an assistant can stand in back of and to one side of the dog (depending on which way she goes to heel) and, after the owner gives the command, the assistant gently taps the dog on the hip with his shoe, to make her start. The owner's praise and the patting of the leg encourage the dog the rest of the way.

Doesn't Do A Complete Finish

Put the dog on leash. Wad the handle of the leash into a ball and hold it in your left hand with elbow straight. Give the command "Robin, heel!" without moving your arm. As the dog moves around to the left side, wait and see if she does an incomplete finish. If she sits at an angle, jerk the leash just as she sits down, to make her move further around. It is important that you give praise after the heel command. Praise encourages a dog to do a complete finish. Praise softens the correction in case the dog sits crooked and you have to correct her.

COMING WHEN CALLED
(The Recall)

Start by teaching your dog to respond to the word "come." With the dog on leash, let her wander at will. When she is sniffing some object, or stands gazing off into the distance, call her name. Tell her "Come," and after you say it, snap the leash once, then clap your hands to encourage her to run to you. Do this until your dog will turn toward you, regardless of what she is doing, when she hears the word "come."

Next, leave her on a sit-stay. Face her the length of the leash. Say her name and tell her "Come!" Use a HAPPY tone of voice. **After** you call her (not **when**), tug on the leash to start her, then clap your hands and praise her while she is coming. After she comes, tell her "Sit," then pat her. Insist upon square sits and as close as possible.

Your dog may start toward you when you call, but then decide to go elsewhere. Change your voice to a demanding "COME!" Follow with one good tug on the leash at the point the dog veers away. The double command of "Come! Come!" is very effective when followed by a leash correction as the dog starts to amble off.

When you take the leash off, use the same HAPPY tone of voice. Follow the command with praise. Even clap your hands enthusiastically until your dog comes willingly. If she wanders off or runs away instead, use the demanding "COME!" If necessary, throw the leash at her heels to make her listen, then kneel and coax her to come. If your dog persists in running away, ask members of your family, and friends, to chase the dog back to you when you call. It is hard, by yourself, to correct a dog that runs wild.

After your dog is dependable, prepare her for the recall as it is done in Obedience Trials. Stand erect when you call her. Make her sit squarely in front after she comes. Have her complete the exercise by going to heel position on command or signal.

RECALL Problems—How To Overcome Them

Doesn't Come On First Command

Ask someone to stand directly in back of your dog. Get the dog's attention, then call her. Follow by clapping your hands and giving praise. If the dog doesn't start, the assistant lightly taps the dog's hindquarters with the toe of his shoe. Clapping the hands will make the dog forget the correction.

Tossing something lightly behind the dog from a hidden source will have the same effect, but take care the dog doesn't see the object thrown nor the person who throws it. Praise and the clapping of the hands will again overcome the correction.

Comes Before She Is Called

Leave your dog. Face her the length of the training area. Hold the rolled-up leash in your hand. If the dog starts before she is called, toss the leash in front to block her. Take her back and try again. In practice, alternate the come with the sit-stay.

Doesn't Sit Close On Recall

At the point where your dog slows down or comes to a sitting position, quietly but firmly repeat "Come, COME, COME!" until she moves forward to sit closer in front. When she does, reward her with a pat or, if she likes to eat, a tasty morsel. To bring the dog closer, use only your voice. Don't move your feet.

Doesn't Do A Complete Finish After She Comes

Put the dog on leash. Wad the leash into a ball and hold it in your left hand. Give the heel command without moving your arm. Let the dog move around to heel position and wait for her to sit at an angle. When she does, jerk the leash backward to make her move further around. Praise when you jerk the leash.

RECALL Problems—How To Overcome Them

Comes Slowly When Called

After you call your dog, turn and RUN. She should instinctively speed up. If she doesn't, ask an assistant to hide where the dog can't see him. When the dog slows to a walk or stops entirely, the assistant drops something in back of the dog to make her run toward the owner. The owner softens the correction by clapping his hands and giving praise, to assure the dog the correction was all in fun.

A slow response on the "come" is usually the result of inadequate praise while training the dog. Until your dog learns to run to you willingly and quickly, give praise with every command. The praise can be dropped after your dog responds with eagerness.

Goes Directly To Heel After Recall

Put your dog on leash. Face her for the recall. Ask an assistant to stand behind you. Call your dog but don't use the leash to make her sit in front. Wait for her to go to heel without sitting. When she does, the assistant drops something directly in front of her. After the correction, gather up the leash, make her sit straight, then praise and pat her. Repeat the exercise but take care the assistant makes the correction ONLY if the dog goes directly to heel without stopping in front. You can make the correction by holding something in your left hand and dropping it in front of the dog.

Crooked Sit On Come

With your dog on leash and sitting in front, hold the leash in BOTH hands. Tell her "Come!" Walk backward and take the dog with you. Halt, wait for the dog to sit at an angle, then pull the leash taut and spank her on whichever hip is out of line. Use either hand. Keep in mind that the dog should start to sit crooked before you correct her, and never correct her without giving praise.

Alternate correction: with the dog on leash, ask two assistants to stand two to three feet apart, and facing one another. Take your position on the third side of the square, facing the dog. After the dog comes, and if she starts to sit crooked, the slightest movement on the part of either assistant should make the dog correct herself and sit straight.

Follows Handler When Left For The Recall Exercise

Carry some object in your left hand. This can be a rolled-up magazine or the leash wadded into a ball. After you leave your dog, if she follows, throw the object backward so it lands in front to block her.

Alternate method: after you leave your dog, turn and face her. Slowly walk backward. If she starts to follow, throw your leash in front of her, then take her back and try again.

LYING DOWN ON COMMAND OR SIGNAL

Keep these two things in mind when you teach your dog to lie down: (1) move slowly, and (2) give continuous praise while you ease the dog into the down position. If she struggles, don't force her. Hold firm until she relaxes, then continue with gentle training. You may have to out-wait your dog ten or fifteen minutes until she decides she will be more comfortable in a prone position than in the one in which you are holding her.

If it is a large dog you are training, face her and play the leash out until it touches the floor. Step over it with your right foot, so it will slide under your instep. When you do this, say "Stay!" (You don't want your dog to take a foot signal.) Take your foot away, then step over the leash again, repeating the word "Stay!" After the dog is sitting quietly, grasp the leash low down with both hands, say "Down," and slowly pull up, giving praise.

Do the same with a small dog, but when you pull up on the leash with the left hand, press on the dog's shoulders with the right hand. At the same time, scratch her shoulders and give praise. (See illustration.)

After your dog lies down on command, teach her to lie down on signal. With the dog on leash, face her (rather close). Put the leash on the ground and stand on it with your left foot (see illustration). Raise your right hand and tell her "Down!" Hold your hand with fingers pointing up while you step on the leash under the dog's chin

Teaching a large stubborn dog to lie down

with your right foot to make her lie down. Praise when you do it. The raised hand in the form of a salute is a signal easily seen at a distance. It is also a signal the dog won't confuse with any other signal. (Lowering the hand as a signal to down, for instance, is similar to the hand motion used when teaching the come, and your dog could be confused.) Use the same signal for a small dog but while teaching her to obey a signal, give it from a crouched position so the hand will be at the eye level of the dog.

Strive for a quick response to your command or signal to lie down. Hold the leash in your left hand, this time just clearing the floor. Raise your right hand and command "Down!" After you give the command, stamp on the leash with your right foot to get immediate action. When working with a small breed or a dog that is sensitive by nature, tap the leash gently. Give praise when you do it. If you are left-handed, follow the same procedure, substituting left for right and right for left.

Some dogs get stubborn when told to lie down. Others resent the command and will leap at the owner. In this case, hold the leash with about six inches dangling free. If the dog lunges forward or refuses to go down, flip the leash once across the tip of her nose, then pull up on the leash until she goes down. When you use the leash, be careful of the eyes. (See illustration.)

Teaching the signal for the DOWN

Hand signal DOWN from the side

Hand signal DOWN from the front.

When teaching your dog to lie down, the important thing is **not to jerk** her to the ground but to ease her to the down position, praising her while you do it.

Teaching a small dog the DOWN

THE DOWN-AT-HEEL POSITION

If you are training your dog for the Novice work in Obedience Trials, the down-at-heel position will prepare your dog for the long down exercise. If you are just a pet owner, you will use the down-at-heel on numerous occasions around the home.

To train your dog to lie down at your left side, place your left hand on the leash, close to the dog's collar. Kneel on your left knee, command "Down," and pull down. While you apply pressure on the collar, give praise. After the dog goes down, say "Stay!" Step on the leash with your left foot to keep the dog down, then stand erect. Give the command "Sit," tug upward on the leash, and after the dog is sitting, pat her. Putting a large dog down this way is safer than reaching over the dog's back, which brings a dog's teeth close to the trainer's face.

Do the same with a small dog but reach in front of your body with the right hand and apply gentle pressure to the shoulders while you pull down on the leash. Hold the small dog close to your body and she will feel secure.

THE DOWN-STAY
(The Long Down)

Now that your dog knows how to lie down, teach her to stay in the down position. With your dog in the down position, directly in front of you, back slowly away. If she gets up without permission, grab the leash quickly and put her down again. After the correction, back away slowly to see if she stays in the down position.

With a small dog, stand over her in a crouched position. Hold both hands close to, but not touching her. If she starts to get up, push her down quickly and tell her "Stay!" After she relaxes, back slowly away.

Circle your dog while she is lying down. Move slowly and if she tries to get up, tap her lightly on the nose or pull down on the leash to make her stay down. Tell her more firmly, "STAY!"

When you leave your dog in the down position when she is at your left side, signal the stay with the left hand and step out on the right foot. When you face her, hold both hands with palms toward the dog's muzzle and with fingers pointing down. If the dog starts toward you, block her and make her back up.

With your dog in the down-stay position, face her and gently pull the leash taut. If the dog uses the tight leash as an excuse to move forward, correct her by putting her down again and telling her in a more severe tone, "STAY!"

DOWN Problems—How To Overcome Them

Ignores Command Or Signal To Lie Down

Put the dog on leash. If it is a large dog, step over the leash with your right foot so it will slide under your instep. Hold the center of the leash in your left hand and the handle in your right hand with about six inches dangling. After you give the command and raise your right hand, flip the end of the leash once against the dog's muzzle. (Be careful of the eyes.) Then pull up on the leash and make the dog lie down.

With a small dog, lean over and after you raise your hand and give the command, bump the dog's nose once with the palm of your hand. After you bump it, press on her shoulders to make her lie down. Pat her!

Dog Creeps On The Down

Give the signal for the down by raising either hand, depending upon whether you are right- or left-handed. Hold your fingers pointing up. If the dog creeps forward, drop your hand quickly and tap her on the nose to make her draw back. After she draws back, pat her. With the small dog, lean over before you give the command or signal so your hand will be close to the dog.

Dog Sits Up When Handler Returns After The Long Down

When you return to your dog and find her sitting, or if she gets up while you are circling, drop your hand quickly and tap her nose. Tell her "DOWN!" After she is lying down, pat her.

Dog Is Slow To Obey The Signal And Command To Lie Down When At Heel Position

Put the dog on leash. Signal the down with the LEFT hand by holding the hand above the leash with wrist bent. Command "Down!" If the dog ignores the command and signal or is slow to obey, snap the dog to a down position by dropping the hand forcefully onto the leash.

DOWN Problems—How To Overcome Them

Dog Rolls Over When Told To Lie Down

After your dog goes down on command or signal, quickly call out "STAY!" Do this before she has a chance to roll over.

Creeps Forward When Made To Sit From The Down

After you give the command or the signal to sit, if the dog moves forward, lift your knee and bump her chest.

With a small dog, use the inside of either foot to bump her and make her draw back.

Dog Sits Up On The Down

Fasten her leash to a ring in the floor or in the ground, with the leash slack enough so the dog can start to get up but can't get to a sitting position. In time, she may correct herself. Try fastening a long line to her collar, then running it through a ring in the ground. You can make a sharper correction by giving a good tug on the line. When the leash is off, ask an assistant to stand close to the dog and tap her on the nose when she lifts herself to a sitting position.

Hand signal STAND from the side

THE STAND

With your dog sitting at heel position, wad the leash into a ball and hold it in your right hand. Place your right hand in front of your dog's muzzle. Reach over the dog's back with the left hand and while you tickle her stomach, pull the leash forward with the right hand, to make her stand. Tell her "Stand!" If she attempts to walk forward, bump her nose gently with the right hand—the hand that is holding the leash. A bump on the nose is effective and it won't make your dog hand-shy.

Next, teach your dog to stand on command while walking at heel position. Hold the leash in your right hand, and before you come to a halt, drop your right hand in front of the dog, tell her "Stand," and at the same time, reach over her back and scratch her stomach. Praise when you do this. Repeat the heeling and the standing-at-heel until the dog will stand by herself when you place your right hand in front of her. By giving the signal to stand with your right hand, you won't confuse the dog with the signal for the stays, where the left hand is used.

Teach your dog to resist pressure. Scratch her back. Push on it. She should brace her feet and stiffen her body. If she sits instead, tap her to a standing position and repeat the command more demandingly. When working with a small dog, loop the handle end of the leash under the dog's stomach to keep her standing.

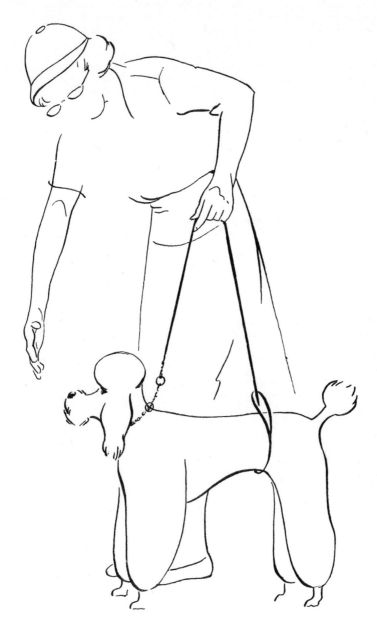

The leash under the stomach works with large dogs as well as small.

THE STAND FOR EXAMINATION

At Obedience Trials, the judge examines each dog individually. Prepare your dog for this test by asking members of your family and strangers to examine the dog during the stand-stay. If she creeps forward, reprimand her sharply by tapping her under the muzzle. Bounce her to a standing position if she sits. If she moves because she is shy or because she is over-friendly, make her pay the consequences for ignoring your command to remain where left. A sharp correction from you will be effective.

The easy way to teach the STAND signal.

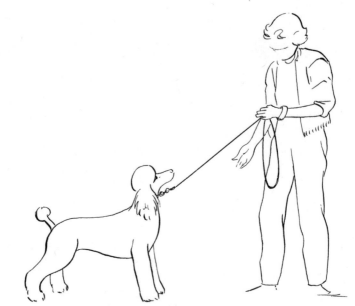

To overcome creeping, pull the leash taut. If the dog moves, tap her under the chin.

THE STAND-STAY

With your dog standing at heel, give the command and signal to stay. If your dog moves forward, correct by reaching backward and bumping her nose with the LEFT hand. If she sits, cuff her from underneath with the same hand.

When your dog will hold the stand, face her and try to pull her from the stand-stay position. When you draw the leash forward, she should brace all feet and refuse to move. If she moves, correct her! Tap her under the muzzle to make her back up, then repeat the stay command.

Circle your dog several times while she is standing. Return to heel by going to the right and around in back. Hold the leash to your left and keep it slack. If the dog moves forward or sits before you give permission, repeat the command in a demanding voice and correct rather sharply.

When you face your dog, hold the palms of both hands toward her muzzle with fingers pointing DOWN.

THE SIT, THE STAND, THE DOWN-AT-HEEL POSITION

Teach your dog the difference between sitting, standing, and lying down at heel position. When you halt, the dog should sit without being told. If she doesn't, spank her to a sitting position or use the leash with a backward snap. The important thing is to have your feet together before you make the correction.

To make her lie down, place your left hand on the leash close to her neck. Command "Down," and pull her head slowly to the ground. Praise when you pull down on the leash.

If you want your dog to stand, while still moving forward, drop your right hand in front of her and say "Stand," and at the same time stroke her back with the left hand or scratch her stomach to keep her standing.

STAND Problems—How To Overcome Them

Won't Stand At Heel

After you loop the leash under your dog's stomach, hold the center of the leash in your left hand (see illustration). While walking, signal the stand with your right hand. Don't pull up on the leash until the dog starts to sit down. Give praise when you lift her to a standing position. If you have a small dog, lift her gently.

Won't Stand For Examination

Loop the handle of a second leash around your dog's stomach. Ask an assistant to stand behind the dog and hold the handle of the leash, but to keep the leash slack. After you tell the dog "Stay," face her. If she tries to sit during the examination or moves forward, call out a second "Stay," after which the assistant should lift her to a standing position or pull backward to keep her from walking forward. The important thing is to call out the command before the assistant takes action.

Dog Shies Away From The Judge

Hold a rolled-up magazine in your hand during the examination. When the dog moves away from the judge, drop the magazine directly in front of her and tell her more firmly, "Stay!" If the judge comes in on the other side, and the dog shies in the opposite direction, drop the magazine there. The point is to block the dog in whichever direction she moves.

Dog Sits When Judge Examines Her

Have your dog straddle some object. For a small dog, this can be an empty coffee can. For the large dog, place a broom handle on the rungs of two chairs. Ask the "judge" to press on the dog's back lightly, forcing her to touch the object with her stomach. This should teach her to stiffen her legs and resist pressure while she is being examined.

STAND Problems—How To Overcome Them

Dog Growls And Snaps During Stand For Examination

Muzzle the dog and then ask three or four people to circle her, all at the same time, without touching her. Later, ask them, one at a time, to stroke her back and give praise. If she shows resentment, tell her in your most demanding voice, "STAY!"

Still later, hold a rolled-up magazine in your hand. If the dog growls, snaps, or moves away, drop the magazine directly in front of her and again tell her "No! Stay!" To make such a dog stay, the dog must be more afraid of the consequences for disobeying the owner's command, than of the judge who examines her.

Dog Sits As Handler Returns After Stand For Examination

After the dog has been examined, return to heel position, wait a few moments, then tell her "Stay," and leave her again. When you return to heel, avoid gathering up the leash, as this may tempt her to sit. When you pat her after the exercise is over, pat her while she is standing.

STICK JUMPING

Stick jumping is a change from the basic routine and dogs enjoy it. It teaches them to jump onto the grooming table, to leap in and out of cars and over small hurdles. It prepares them for advanced training, which includes jumping obstacles.

A sawed-off broom handle or a piece of dowling thirty inches long, will serve as a jumping stick. Hold the stick in your right hand. Wad the handle end of the leash into a ball and carry it in your left hand. Place the end of the stick against a stationary object, such as a tree or a post, but keep it LOW. The dog will eventually jump the equal of one and a half times her shoulder height, but while she is learning, hold the stick only a few inches above the ground and keep all hurdles low to the ground.

Give the jumping command, which can be "Over," "Hup," or "Jump," then pull the leash over the stick, ahead of the dog. While she is jumping, tell her "Good girl!" If she braces all four feet and refuses to jump, lay the stick on the floor or the ground, then slowly drag her over the stick, giving praise while you do it. If you allow your dog to balk at a jump, she will form a habit that is hard to break.

Next, teach the dog the jumping command. After she learns to jump freely, place the stick in front of her, command "Jump," and after you say it, give the leash a forward snap. While you are snapping the leash, give praise. It is important that you say the word "jump" before you tug on the leash.

When you take the leash off, after you place the stick, point to it with your left hand when you tell your dog to jump.

Stick Jumping

GENERAL Problems—How To Overcome Them

Dog Takes Judge's Commands

In practice, have someone call out the judge's command. Count five before you tell your dog what to do.

If you train by yourself, give the judge's commands aloud before you give the commands to the dog. This will teach your dog not to respond to the sound of the voice but to wait for definite words.

Dog Runs Away During Training

If your dog darts away while heeling, reach out and slap her across the rump to make her look around. If it is a small dog, drop something at her heels. Repeat the heel command, using a more demanding tone. Follow by patting your side and giving praise.

If the dog ignores your command to "come" and runs playfully about, throw something at her heels when she isn't looking, then drop to a kneeling position, call her and offer protection.

Teaching a dog to go to the person who calls, should be a family affair. At home and in the training area, cooperate by pointing to the person who called the dog and telling her "GO!" Chase her if necessary. To correct the dog that won't come when called, station one or two assistants in different parts of the training area, and arm them with an empty carton or two. When the dog ignores the command to "come," ask those who are assisting, to block the dog by dropping the carton in front of her, in order to drive her back to the person who called. In the meantime, the one who called the dog should kneel, clap his hands, give praise and offer the dog protection.

Anticipates Commands

Avoid following a set routine. For instance, alternate the come with the sit-stay. If your dog anticipates the "finish," pivot back on your left foot to heel position and don't let her complete the exercise. Each time she moves without permission, tell her "Stay" more emphatically.

Dog Whines During Sit- And Down-Stays

The following suggestions may lessen the whining, but may not be a complete cure:

Train your dog to stay alone, as much as possible.

Muzzle the dog temporarily, with a piece of gauze bandage. When she is quiet, take the bandage off. When she whines, put it on.

Consult your veterinarian. Ask if he recommends a tranquilizer to calm your dog's nerves.

Finally, buy a little water gun. Squirt water at her from the distance, every time she starts to whine.

A dog that has learned to stay alone will be less inclined to whine or to break on the stays than the dog that always has company. Train your dog to be independent so she will feel secure when you leave her.

Dog Loses Points For Sniffing

Make it a rule never to let your dog put her nose to the ground unless you give her permission. When she is on leash, whether she is walking, sitting, or standing, jerk up on the leash when the head goes down. When you enter the show grounds, be unusually strict about this. If you want her to exercise, give her a command such as "duties," or release her with an "O.K."

Dog Is Inattentive

In practice, turn unexpectedly during the heeling exercise or spank your dog playfully when she looks away. When you want her to come, don't wait for her to look at you before you call her. Give the command, then tug on the leash, whether she is looking at you or not. If she looks away during the stand, the sit, or the down-stays, yell "Hey," when she turns her head away. Use food to entice her if she is a dog that likes to eat.

GRADUATION

Requirements for receiving a diploma after a nine or ten weeks' training course: *

Dog to heel on a slack leash and to be under control at all times. Dog to sit automatically when handler halts.

Dog to stay for one minute in the sitting position, without a second command. Handler approximately fifteen feet away.

Dog to stay for one minute in the down position, without a second command. Handler approximately fifteen feet away.

Dog to hold the stand-stay position, without a second command. Handler holds the leash in his hand.

Dog to heel; alternate the sit-at-heel with the down-at-heel and stand-at-heel positions.

Dog to respond to the down, the come, and the "finish" (going to heel position) when both command and signal are used.

Dog to heel with leash over the handler's shoulder. Possibly, for the final test, the leash removed.

---

* Note: these are not the requirements for the Novice Class at an AKC licensed Obedience Trial but suggested requirements after a nine or ten weeks' training class.

Heeling and Sitting List good workers	Stays List Breaks			Sitting Lying down Standing at Heel List good workers	Quick Response to			Heeling Leash over Shoulder List good workers	Stick Jumping List good workers	Free Heeling List good workers	Remarks for Special Handling Award
	Sit	Stand	Down		Down	Come	Finish				
1				1	2	2	2	1		1	2 very difficult dog good handling
3	3		3					3		3	
4				4	4	4	4	4	4	4	
5		5		5	5	5	5	5	5	5	5 good handling dog no problem
6	6			6	6			6	6	6	

Best Performance

Prize	First	Second	Third	Fourth
Dog. No.	4	5	6	1

Handling Award

Dog No. 2

Note: When a number appears in every column except the Sit, the Down and the Stand Stays, the dog should not be overlooked for placement among the winners.

Sample judging chart for a group graduation

SUGGESTIONS FOR
EXHIBITING IN THE NOVICE OBEDIENCE CLASSES

Give your dog sufficient training, so you will feel confident when you enter the Obedience ring.

Read the Obedience "rule book" * carefully and familiarize yourself with the show ring procedure. The extra commands and signals, and body gestures you used to train your dog, are not permitted in a regular trial. Carelessness in handling could cause your dog to fail. When the rules do not forbid the second command, give an extra one if necessary and take a penalty. Permissible corrections at shows will keep a dog from getting ringwise.

In practice, train your dog in unfamiliar surroundings. When she gets to the show, she will be less distracted.

When you enter the show grounds, keep your dog from sniffing. Every time she lowers her head, jerk up on the leash to make her pay attention. Sniffing is a major problem of Obedience exhibitors.

The majority of dogs are at their best when they have been left alone, prior to competing. Staying by herself for only a few moments may alert your dog, and make her anxious to please.

Exercise and give your dog a drink of water before your turn comes

---

* *Regulations and Standards for Obedience Trials* available from:
The American Kennel Club, 51 Madison Ave., New York, N.Y.
The Canadian Kennel Club, 667 Yonge St., Toronto 5, Canada.
Obedience rules are revised occasionally. Make certain you have the latest copy.

to enter the ring. If the dog is to do her best work, she must feel comfortable. Groom her for appearances' sake!

Take time and observe the judging procedure for the day. A judge usually follows the same pattern for each exhibitor. If, while working, you fail to hear a command, you will have some idea of where to go, because you watched the routine.

When you are in the Obedience ring, walk briskly and move in a straight line. Keep your corners square and when you do an about-turn, pivot smoothly, without fancy footwork. Some handlers take a step backward before they turn, and this leaves the dog behind.

When the judge calls for a "FAST," change to a running pace. Don't just walk a little faster. In the SLOW, avoid sauntering or your dog will want to sit down. When it is time for the Figure 8, take your position, facing the judge. If the judge wants you to go a certain way, he will tell you. If not, select whichever way you please. While doing the Figure 8, walk naturally and let the dog change pace.

In the Obedience ring, THE STAND FOR EXAMINATION is done off lead. The leash is removed, and given to the steward. After you stand your dog, either by posing her or by giving a command or signal, stand erect yourself, then automatically give the command and signal to stay, and leave her.

When you leave your dog for THE RECALL, go where the judge tells you, but avoid standing with your back against the rope or barrier, or close to objects such as the judge's table or chair. Carelessness in selecting a place to stand can cause your dog to do an incomplete "finish." When you give the command to "come," keep your voice HAPPY. If there is a great deal of noise, yell the command louder than usual.

During the LONG SIT and LONG DOWN exercises, place your armband and leash far enough away so your dog won't be tempted to sniff them. If it is the LONG SIT, have your dog sitting squarely on both hips. If it is the LONG DOWN, leave her resting comfortably on one hip. Note that you cannot use your hands to position or down your dog. Give the command and signal together, but don't use your dog's your right foot from an upright position. Crouching encourages a dog to follow.

While you are away from your dog, don't fidget. Your dog may interpret the slightest body or hand motion as a signal to come.

When you return to your dog after the sit- or down-stays, take care not to step on her or bump her accidentally. By the same token, be considerate of your competitor's dog.

In practice, train your dog to lie down at heel position when you give a signal with your left hand. This looks well in the ring and if you have an excitable dog to handle, you can keep her under control more easily between exercises.

After your dog's performance in the Obedience ring, if you are pleased with the way she worked, don't be ashamed to show it. If you aren't pleased, let the ringside think you are anyway! Obedience is a sporting game, not to be taken too seriously.

BE PROUD OF YOUR TRAINED DOG.
MAKE HER A CREDIT TO OBEDIENCE.

For more detailed instructions on training your dog, see:

The Complete Book of Dog Obedience, by Blanche Saunders (Howell Book House)

Training You To Train Your Dog, by Blanche Saunders (Doubleday)

The Complete Open Obedience Course, by Blanche Saunders (Howell Book House)

The Complete Utility Obedience Course, by Blanche Saunders (Howell Book House)

Also, see:

The New Standard Book of Dog Care and Training, by Jeannette W. Cross and Blanche Saunders (Howell Book House)

Dog Training for Boys and Girls, by Blanche Saunders (Howell Book House)

Grooming and Showing Instructions (Howell Book House)